How to Raise and Train a

# DOBERMAN
# PINSCHER

# By Natalie Stebbins
# and Sara M. Barbaresi

Distributed in the U.S.A. by T.F.H. Publications, Inc., 211 West Sylvania Avenue, P.O. Box 27, Neptune City, N.J. 07753; in England by T.F.H. (Gt. Britain) Ltd., 13 Nutley Lane, Reigate, Surrey; in Canada by Clarke, Irwin & Company, Clarwin House, 791 St. Clair Avenue West, Toronto 10, Ontario; in Southeast Asia by Y. W. Ong, 9 Lorong 36 Geylang, Singapore 14; in Australia and the south Pacific by Pet Imports Pty. Ltd., 38-40 Chard Road, Brookvale 2100, N.S.W., Australia.
The U.S.A. book trade distributors are Crown Publishers, Inc., 419 Park Avenue South, New York, N.Y. 10016.

**ACKNOWLEDGMENTS**

*Three Lions* photographed the Doberman Pinschers owned by Mr. and Mrs. J. Monroe Stebbins, Jr., 2 Choir Lane, Westbury, L.I., N.Y. and Fred Wickel of Wantagh, L.I. Berman Briar, Grand Victor, 1957, whose picture appears on page 4 , is owned by Bernard Berman, Box 28, Southfields, N.Y. Ch. Dortmund Delly's Colonel Jet and Ch. Steb's Top Skipper are owned by the Stebbins.

# CONTENTS

Berman Briar, Grand Victor, 1957, is every inch a champion.

# 1. Doberman Pinscher Standards

The Doberman Pinscher is a "new" dog as breeds go, and a relative newcomer to this country. The Doberman's nobility, courage and gallantry shown during the war, and his devotion to home and family have won him a lasting place in the affections of America's dog lovers.

In spite of his bold, alert look of powerful readiness and his reputation as a guard and police dog, the Doberman is a gentleman, and an affectionate, obedient pet. Like any intelligent dog with natural working ability, however, he needs training. If you spend ten minutes a day training your Doberman, you will have a dog to be proud of.

## HISTORY OF THE BREED

The Doberman is an unusual breed in that one man is credited with its development. Pinscher is the German word meaning terrier, and the breed is probably descended from terrier-type dogs of the region of Thueringen, in Germany. Herr Louis Dobermann, the dogcatcher of the town of Apolda, gave his name to the breed (the second N was dropped in America), but probably his dogs were only one family of a local type. The black-and-tan pinscher, shepherd and hunting dogs, and possibly the Rottweil butcher's dog are in the breed's ancestry.

Another of the first Doberman breeders, Otto Goeller, contributed greatly to the development of a uniform type and standard. He formed the first breed club in 1899, and it was recognized the following year. Dobermans were first recognized in the United States in 1908, but the Doberman Pinscher Club of America was not founded until 1927. Since then it has been an active sponsor of the breed, holding an annual specialty in different parts of the country, with many local clubs as well.

Black-and-tan was the first recognized color, but the rich red-brown and rarer blue, both with the same distinctive tan or rust markings, are also popular.

The Doberman is now twenty-first in American Kennel Club rankings of breeds, with slightly under 4000 registrations a year during the last ten years. It is a healthy sign of breed popularity to maintain figures on such a level with no sudden spurt of favor, which, with other breeds, has been too often followed by failure to keep up high standards of type and temperament.

Notable attention has increased the Doberman's popularity, however. Adopted as the official dog of the U.S. Marine Corps, it served with often-commended bravery as a sentry and trailing dog. Trained guards and trackers are used by stores, schools and sheriffs. Several guide dog schools use Dobermans exclusively or in company with other dogs adapted to this most difficult task of a trained dog.

In the show ring too the Doberman has won fame and made friends for his breed. Ch. Rancho Dobe's Storm made headlines by winning first place at the most important of all shows, Westminster, twice in a row, a record equalled by only three other dogs. Other Dobermans that have added to the breed's show ring laurels include the leading sires Ch. Dictator v Glengugel and Ch. Delegate v d Elbe. The outstanding best-in-show winner Ch. Dortmund Delly's Colonel Jet and Ch. Braun's Eric head the list of today's living sires. Producer of many champions, the distaff side is led by Siegerin (Germany's top winner of the year) and Ch. Jessy v d Sonnenhoehe, and the recent brood matron Meadowmist Isis of Ahrtal.

## BREED SPECIFICATIONS

The standard by which the Doberman is judged, drawn up by the Doberman Pinscher Club of America (E. A. Black, secretary, 2653 Rosebud Lane, Fort Worth, Texas) and approved by the Board of Directors of the American Kennel Club, follows:

GENERAL CONFORMATION AND APPEARANCE — The appearance is that of a dog of good middle size, with a body that is square, the height measured vertically from the ground to the highest point of the withers, equaling the length, measured horizontally, from the forechest to the rear projection of the upper thigh. Height at the withers — males 26 to 28 inches, ideal being about 27 inches; bitches 24 to 26 inches, ideal being about 25½ inches. Compactly built, muscular and powerful, for great endurance and speed. Elegant in appearance, of proud carriage, reflecting great nobility and temperament. Energetic, watchful, determined, alert, fearless, loyal and obedient.

*Faults:* Coarseness. Fine Greyhound build. Undersized or oversized. *Disqualifying faults:* Shyness, viciousness. Shyness: a dog shall be judged fundamentally shy if, refusing to stand for examination, it shrinks away from the judge; if it fears an approach from the rear; if it shies at sudden and unusual noises to a marked degree. Viciousness: a dog that attacks, or attempts to attack, either the judge or its handler, is definitely vicious. An aggressive or belligerent attitude toward other dogs shall not be deemed viciousness.

HEAD SHAPE — Long and dry, resembling a blunt wedge, both frontal

**Ch. Dortmund Delly's Colonel Jet was an outstanding best-in-show winner.**

and profile views. When seen from the front the head widens gradually toward the base of the ears in a practically unbroken line. Top of skull flat, turning with slight stop to bridge of muzzle, with muzzle line extending parallel to the top line of the skull. Cheeks flat and muscular. Lips lying close to jaws, and not drooping. Jaws full and powerful, well filled under the eyes. Nose, solid black in black dogs, dark brown in brown ones, and dark gray in blues.

*Faults:* Head out of balance in proportion to body. Ram's, dishfaced, cheeky or snipey heads.

EYES — Almond-shaped, not round, moderately deep set, not prominent, with vigorous, energetic expression. Iris of uniform color, ranging from medium to darkest brown in black dogs, the darker shade being the more desirable. In reds or blues, the color of the iris should blend with that of the markings, but not be of a lighter hue than that of the markings.

*Faults:* Slit eyes. Glassy eyes.

TEETH — Strongly developed and white. Lower incisors upright and touching inside of upper incisors — a true scissors bite. Forty-two teeth (22 in lower jaw, 20 in upper jaw). Distemper teeth should not be penalized.

*Disqualifying faults:* Overshot more than 3/16 of an inch. Undershot more than 1/8 of an inch.

EARS — Well-trimmed and carried erect. (In all states where ear trimming is prohibited, or where dogs with cropped ears cannot be shown, the foregoing requirements are waived.) The upper attachment of the ears, when held erect, should be on a level with the top of the skull.

NECK — Carried upright, well muscled and dry. Well arched, and with nape of neck widening gradually toward body. Length of neck proportionate to body and head.

BODY — *Back* short, firm, of sufficient width, and muscular at the loin extending in a straight line from withers to the slightly rounded croup. *Withers* pronounced and forming the highest point of body. *Brisket* full and broad, reaching deep to the elbow. *Chest* broad, and forechest well defined. *Spring of ribs* pronounced. *Belly* well tucked up, extending in a curved line from chest. *Loins* wide and muscled. *Hips* broad in proportion to body, breadth of hips being approximately breadth of body at rib spring. *Tail,* docked at approximately second joint, should appear to be the continuation of the spine, without material drop.

FOREQUARTERS — Shoulder blade and upper arm should meet at an angle of 90 degrees. Relative length of shoulder and upper arm should be as one to one, excess length of upper arm being much less undesirable than excess length of shoulder blade. *Legs,* seen from the front and side, perfectly straight and parallel to each other from elbow to pastern; muscled and sinewy with round, heavy bone. In a normal position and when gaiting the elbow should lie close to the brisket. *Pasterns* firm, with an almost perpendicular position to the ground. *Feet* well arched, compact and catlike, turning neither in nor out.

HINDQUARTERS — In balance with forequarters. Upper shanks long, wide and well-muscled on both sides of thigh, with clearly defined stifle. While the dog is at rest, hock to heel should be perpendicular to the ground. Upper shanks, lower shanks and hocks should be parallel to each other, and wide enough apart to fit in with a properly built body. The hipbone should fall away from the spinal column at an angle of about 30 degrees. The upper shank should be at right angles to the hip bone. Croup well filled out. Cat-feet, as on front legs, turning neither in nor out.

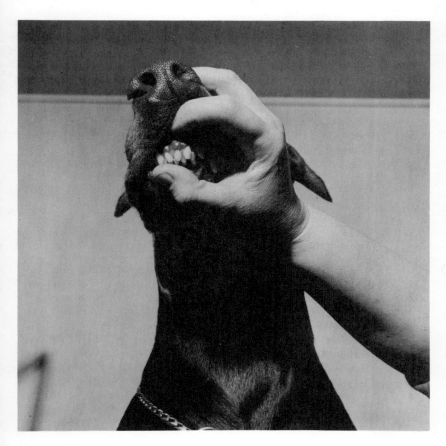

**The Doberman's teeth should be strong and white, with a true scissors bite.**

GAIT — The gait should be free, balanced and vigorous, with good reach in the forequarters and good driving power in the hindquarters. When trotting there should be a strong rear-action drive, with rotary motion of hindquarters. Each rear leg should move in line with the foreleg on the same side. Rear and front legs should be thrown neither in nor out. Back should remain strong, firm and level.

COAT, COLOR, MARKINGS — *Coat:* smooth-haired, short, hard, thick and close-lying. Invisible grey undercoat on neck permitted. *Allowed colors:* black, brown or blue. *Markings:* rust red, sharply defined, and appearing above each eye, and on muzzle, throat and forechest, and on all legs and feet, and below tail. White on chest, not exceeding one-half square inch, permissible.

9

The foregoing description is that of the ideal Doberman Pinscher. Any deviation from the above-described dog must be penalized in proportion to the extent of the deviation, and in accordance with the appended scale of points.

*Scale of Points*

*General Conformation and Appearance*

| | |
|---|---:|
| Proportions | 8 |
| Bone Substance | 8 |
| Temperament, Expression, Nobility | 8 |
| Condition | 5 |
| Total | 29 |

*Head*

| | |
|---|---:|
| Shape | 6 |
| Teeth | 5 |
| Eyes | 3 |
| Ears | 1 |
| Total | 15 |

*Neck* .................... 3

*Body*

| | |
|---|---:|
| Backline, Withers, Loins, Tail Placement | 8 |
| Chest, Brisket, Rib Spring, Tuck Up | 8 |
| Shape and Proportion | 4 |
| Total | 20 |

*Forequarters*

| | |
|---|---:|
| Shoulders, Upper Arms, Legs, Pasterns | 5 |
| Angulation | 4 |
| Paws | 2 |
| Total | 11 |

*Hindquarters*

| | |
|---|---:|
| Upper Thigh, Stifle, Hocks | 5 |
| Angulation | 4 |
| Paws | 2 |
| Total | 11 |

*Gait* .................... 6

*Coat, Color, Markings* .................... 5

GRAND TOTAL .................... 100

# 2. Buying Your Doberman

Probably you decided that you want a Doberman Pinscher after seeing one of this elegant, impressive breed. If a neighbor's dog had puppies which entranced you or your children, and the puppies are for sale, your task is an easy one. But more likely you just decided that the Doberman was the dog for you, and now you have to find the right one.

First, make up your mind what you want: male or female, adult or puppy, show dog or "just a pet." There is no greater use for a dog than being "just" a beloved pet and companion, but the dog which has profitable show and breeding possibilities is worth more to the seller.

## PET OR SHOW DOG?

The puppy with a slight flaw in his ear carriage or quantity of coat will make just as good a companion and guardian, but his more perfect litter-mate will cost more.

That is why there is often a difference in price between puppies which look—to you, anyway—identical. If you think you may want to show your dog or raise a litter of puppies for the fun of it later on, by all means buy the best you can afford. You will save expense and disappointment later on. However, if the puppy is *strictly* a pet for the children, or companion for you, you can afford to look for a bargain. The pup which is not show material; the older pup, for which there is often less demand; or the grown dog, not up to being used for breeding, are occasionally available and are opportunities to save money. Remember that these are the only real bargains in buying a dog. It takes good food and care—and plenty of both—to raise a healthy, vigorous puppy.

The price you pay for your dog is little compared to the love and devotion he will return over the many years he'll be with you. With good care and affection your pup should live to a ripe old age; through modern veterinary science and nutrition, dogs are better cared for and living longer.

A child and puppy belong together, but the puppy should be protected from teasing and overtiring.

## MALE OR FEMALE?

If you should intend breeding your dog in the future, by all means buy a female. You can find a suitable mate without difficulty when the time comes, and have the pleasure of raising a litter of pups—there is nothing cuter than a fat, playful puppy. If you don't want to raise puppies, your female can be spayed, and will remain a healthy, lively pet. The female is smaller than the male and generally quieter. She has less tendency to roam in search of romance, but a properly trained male can be a charming pet, and has a certain difference in temperament that is appealing to many people Male vs. female is chiefly a matter of personal choice.

## ADULT OR PUP?

Whether to buy a grown dog or a small puppy is another question. It is undeniably fun to watch your dog grow all the way from a baby, sprawling and playful, to a mature, dignified dog. If you don't have the time to spend on the more frequent meals, housebreaking, and other training a puppy needs in order to become a dog you can be proud of, then choose an older, partly trained pup or a grown dog. If you want a show dog, remember that no one, not even an expert, can predict with 100% accuracy what a small puppy will be when he grows up. Someone familiar with dogs may be right *most* of the time, but six months is the earliest age for the would-be exhibitor to pick a prospect and know that his future is relatively safe.

If you have a small child it is best to get a puppy big enough to protect himself, one not less than four or five months old. Older children will enjoy playing with and helping to take care of a baby pup, but at less than four months a puppy wants to do little but eat and sleep, and he must be protected from teasing and overtiring. You cannot expect a very young child to understand that a puppy is a fragile living being; to the youngster he is a toy like a stuffed dog.

## WHERE TO BUY

You can choose among several places to buy your dog. One is a kennel which breeds show dogs as a business and has extra pups for sale as pets. Another is the one-dog owner who wants to sell the puppies from an occasional litter and thus pay his expenses. Pet shops usually buy puppies from overstocked kennels or part-time hobbyists for re-sale, and you can generally buy a puppy there at a reasonable price. To find any of these, watch the pet column of your local newspaper or look in the classified section of your phone book. If you or your friends go driving out in the countryside, be on the lookout for a sign announcing purebred puppies for sale.

Whichever source you try, you can usually tell in a very short time whether the puppies will make healthy and happy pets. If they are clean, fat and lively, they are probably in good health. At the breeder's you will have the advantage of seeing the puppies' mother and perhaps the father and other relatives. Remember that the mother, having just raised a demanding family, won't be looking her best, but if she is sturdy, friendly and well-mannered, her puppies should be, too. If you feel that something is lacking in the care or condition of the dogs, it is better to look elsewhere than to buy hastily and regret it afterward.

You may be impatient to bring home your new dog, but a few days will make little difference in his life with you. Often it is a good idea to choose a puppy and put a deposit on him, but wait to take him home until you have prepared for the new arrival. For instance, it is better for the Christmas puppy to be settled in his new home before the holidays, or else to wait until things have settled down afterward. You may want to wait until the puppy has completed his "shots," and if this is arranged in advance, it is generally agreeable.

If you cannot find the dog you want locally, write to the secretary of the Doberman Pinscher Club of America, Mr. E. A. Black, 2653 Rosebud Lane, Fort Worth, Texas, or to the A.K.C. (page 15), for names of breeders near you, or to whom you can write for information. Puppies are often bought by mail from reputable breeders.

## WHAT TO LOOK FOR IN A PUPPY

In choosing your puppy, assuming that it comes from healthy, well-bred parents, look for one that is friendly and outgoing. The biggest pup in the litter is apt to be somewhat overgrown or clumsy as a grown dog, while the appealing "poor little runt" may turn out to be a timid shadow—or have a Napoleon complex! If you want a show dog and have no experience in choosing the prospect, study the standard (page 6), but be advised by the breeder on the finer points of conformation. His prices will be in accord with the puppies' expected worth, and he will be honest with you because it is to his own advantage. He wants his good puppies placed in the public eye to reflect glory on him—and to attract future buyers.

Your puppy's ears will probably have been cropped when you buy him, as this is usually done at about eight weeks. They may still be wound in tape, to allow the edges to heal and to train them to stand erect. After the tape is removed the puppy's ears should stand erect and add to the graceful look of his head. His tail will have been docked to a short stub when he was a few days old.

The puppy should have bright eyes, dark brown in color, with a keen expression, and without too much haw, or inner eyelid, showing in the corner. His neck should be long and arched, and his body should be deep and short in appearance, on straight, solid-boned legs so that he looks balanced. His muscles will develop as he grows, but he should not look at all spindly or pot-bellied. His coat should be shiny, flat and fine, black as glossy jet, with markings clearly defined deep rust, and red rather than faded looking. His back should be neither sway nor arched, and his tail should come straight out. Hindquarters should be broad and substantial, with hind legs straight when seen from the rear, and with enough angulation from the side. Feet should be short and strong looking. Discounting the bigger bones and tummy, at three months the puppy will greatly resemble a grown dog in miniature. When he moves he will still show puppy gawkiness and looseness of the joints, which tighten with maturity and sufficient exercise. However, he should be able to reach ahead and move true, walking in a straight line and putting one foot behind the other, not paddling or turning out his feet as he lands.

Friendly puppies respond well to gentle handling. The taped ears of the two on the right don't seem to bother them.

## PAPERS

When you buy your puppy you should receive his pedigree and registration certificate or application. These have nothing to do with licensing, which is a local regulation applying to purebred and mongrel alike. Find out the local ordinance in regard to age, etc., buy a license, and keep it on your dog whenever he is off your property.

Your dog's pedigree is a chart, for your information only, showing his ancestry. It is not part of his official papers. The registration certificate is the important part. If the dog was named and registered by his breeders you will want to complete the transfer and send it, with the fee of $1.00, to the American Kennel Club, 221 Fourth Ave., New York 3, N. Y. They will transfer the dog to your ownership in their records, and send a new certificate to you.

If you receive, instead, an application for registration, you should fill it out, choosing a name for your pup, and mail it with the fee of $2.00 to the A.K.C. Be sure that the number of the puppy's litter is included.

# 3. Care of the Doberman Puppy

## BRINGING YOUR PUPPY HOME

When you bring your puppy home, remember that he is used to the peace and relative calm of a life of sleeping, eating and playing with his brothers and sisters. The trip away from all this is an adventure in itself, and so is adapting to a new home. So let him take it easy for awhile. Don't let the whole neighborhood pat and poke him at one time. Be particularly careful when children want to handle him, for they cannot understand the difference between the delicate living puppy and the toy dog they play with and maul. If the puppy is to grow up loving children and taking care of them, he must not get a bad first impression.

## THE PUPPY'S BED

It is up to you to decide where the puppy will sleep. Unless it is winter in a cold climate, even a young puppy can sleep outside in a snug, well-built dog house. It should have a tight, pitched roof to let the rain run off, and a floor off the ground, to avoid dampness. The door should be no larger than the grown dog will need to go in and out, as a bigger opening lets in too much draft. For bedding you can use an old rag or blanket, straw, or sweet-smelling cedar shavings. Whether the puppy sleeps indoors or out, will benefit from an outdoor run of his own where he can be put to exercise and amuse himself. It does not have to be large for if he goes for walks and plays with you he will get enough exercise that way. He is much safer shut in his run than being left loose to follow a stray dog off your property and get into bad habits—if he isn't hit by a car first!

Of course if the dog is left in his run for any length of time he should have protection from the cold, rain or sun. The run should be rectangular, and as big as you can conveniently make it, up to 20 x 40 feet, with strong wire fence which will keep your dog in and intruders out. The wire should be at least four feet high, as many dogs like to jump, and the gate should be fastened with a spring hook or hasp which is not likely to be unfastened by mischance.

If your dog sleeps indoors, he should have his own place, and not be allowed to climb all over the furniture. He should sleep out of drafts, but not right next to the heat, which would make him too sensitive to the cold when he goes outside. If your youngster wants to share his bed with the puppy, that is all right, too, but the puppy must learn the difference between his bed and other furniture. Or he may sleep on a dog bed or in a box big enough to curl up in: a regulation dog crate or one made from a packing box, with bedding for comfort. If your cellar is dry and fairly warm the puppy will be all right there, or in the garage.

You have already decided where the puppy will sleep before you bring him home. Let him stay there, or in the corner he will soon learn is "his," most of the time, so that he will gain a sense of security from the familiar. Give the puppy a little milk with bread and kibble in it when he arrives, but don't worry if he isn't hungry at first. He will soon develop an appetite when he grows accustomed to his surroundings. The first night the puppy may cry a bit from lonesomeness, but if he has an old blanket or rug to curl up in he will be cozy. In winter a hot water bottle will help replace the warmth of his littermates, or the ticking of a clock may provide company.

## FEEDING YOUR PUPPY

It is best to use the feeding schedule to which the puppy is accustomed, and stick to it except when you feel you can modify or improve it. You will probably want to feed the puppy on one of the commercially prepared dog foods as a base, adding meat, fat and a vitamin-mineral supplement, and table scraps when you have them. Remember that the dog food companies have prepared their food so that it is a balanced ration in itself, and, indeed, many dogs are raised on dog food alone. If you try to change this balance too much you are likely to upset your pet's digestion, and the dog will not be as well fed in the long run. Either kibble or meal is a good basic food, and the most economical way to feed your dog.

Milk is good for puppies and some grown dogs like it. Big bones are fine to chew on, especially for teething puppies, but small bones such as chicken, chop or fish bones are always dangerous; they may splinter or stick in the digestive tract. Table scraps such a meat, fat, or vegetables will furnish variety and vitamins, but fried or starchy foods such as potatoes and beans will not be of much food value. Adding a tablespoonful of fat (lard or drippings) to the daily food will keep your puppy's skin healthy and make his coat shine.

Remember that all dogs are individuals. The amount that will keep your dog in good health is right for him, not the "rule-book" amount. A feeding chart to give you some idea of what the average puppy will eat follows:

Doberman puppies are content to eat together from one dish, but make sure each gets his proper share.

WEANING TO 3 MONTHS: *A.M.*—1 cup of dog food, mixed with warm water. *Noon*—1 cup warm milk, with cereal, kibble or biscuits. *P.M.*—½ cup dog food, ¼ tbs. meat, 1 tbs. fat; scraps. *Bedtime*—1 cup warm milk, biscuit.

3-6 MONTHS: *A.M.*—2 cups dog meal or kibble mixed with water. *Noon*—1 cup milk, soft-boiled egg twice a week. *P.M.*—1 cup meal, ¾-1 lb. meat; fat, scraps.

6 MONTHS-1 YEAR: *A.M.*—3 cups dog meal, or milk with kibble. *P.M.*—3 cups dog meal with 1 lb. meat, fat, scraps.

OVER 1 YEAR: *A.M.*—Half of evening meal if you prefer. *P.M.*—4-5 cups meal with 1 lb. meat.

You can try a system of self-feeding instead of giving your puppy regular meals. This means keeping the dry meal or kibble in front of him all the time. If he is inclined to overeat, put out only the daily amount each morning. Otherwise you can leave a filled dish or pail (protected from the weather and insects if outside) where he can nibble at leisure.

You can feed meat, milk, fat, eggs, etc. as a regular meal in addition, too. Remember to increase these amounts as the puppy grows, as long as he continues to clean up each meal and look for the next.

## HOUSEBREAKING YOUR PUPPY

As soon as you get your puppy you can begin to housebreak him but remember that you can't expect too much of him until he is five months old or so. A baby puppy just cannot control himself, so it is best to give him an opportunity to relieve himself before the need arises.

Don't let the puppy wander through the whole house; keep him in one or two rooms under your watchful eye. If he sleeps in the house and has been brought up on newspapers, keep a couple of pages handy on the floor. When he starts to whimper, puts his nose to the ground or runs around looking restless, take him to the paper before an "accident" occurs. After he has behaved, praise him and let him roam again. It is much better to teach him the right way than to punish him for misbehaving. Puppies are

**If you put down newspaper in the puppy's area, if you let him know what is expected of him, and praise him when he obeys, paper training will be easy.**

naturally clean and can be housebroken easily, given the chance. If a mistake should occur, and mistakes are bound to happen occasionally, wash the spot immediately with tepid water, followed by another rinse with water to which a few drops of vinegar have been added. A dog will return to the same place if there is any odor left, so it is important to remove all traces.

If your puppy sleeps outside, housebreaking will be even easier. Remember that the puppy has to relieve himself after meals and whenever he wakes up, as well as sometimes in between. So take him outside as soon as he shows signs of restlessness indoors, and stay with him until he has performed. Then praise and pat him, and bring him back inside as a reward. Since he is used to taking care of himself outdoors, he will not want to misbehave in the house, and will soon let you know when he wants to go out.

You can combine indoor paper training and outdoor housebreaking by taking the puppy out when convenient and keeping newspaper available for use at other times. As the puppy grows older he will be able to control himself for longer periods. If he starts to misbehave in the house, without asking to go out first, scold him and take him out or to his paper. Punishment *after* the fact will accomplish nothing; the puppy cannot understand why he is being scolded unless it is immediate.

The older puppy or grown dog should be able to remain overnight in the house without needing to go out, unless he is ill. If your dog barks or acts restless, take him out once, but unless he relieves himself right away, take him back indoors and shut him in his quarters. No dog will soil his bed if he can avoid it, and your pet will learn to control himself overnight if he has to.

## VETERINARY CARE

You will want your puppy to be protected against the most serious puppyhood diseases: distemper and infectious hepatitis. So your first action after getting him will be to take him to your veterinarian for his shots and a check-up, if he has not already received them. He may have had all or part of the immunization as early as two months of age, so check with the seller before you bring your puppy home.

You may give the puppy temporary serum which provides immunity for about two weeks, but nowadays permanent vaccine providing lifelong immunity can be given so early that the serum is seldom used, except as a precaution in outbreaks. The new vaccine is a combined prevention against distemper and hepatitis, and may be given in one or three shots (two weeks apart). Your veterinarian probably has a preferred type, so go along with him, as either method is protective in a very high percentage of cases.

There is now an effective anti-rabies vaccine, which you can give to your dog if there should be an outbreak of this disease in your neighborhood. It is not permanent, however, so unless local regulations demand it, there is little value in giving the vaccine in ordinary circumstances.

Scold your puppy when he makes a mistake; then take him outdoors or to his paper. Be sure to remove all traces from the floor.

## WORMING

Your puppy has probably been wormed at least once, since puppies have a way of picking up worms, particularly in a kennel where they are exposed to other dogs. Find out when he was last wormed and the date, if any, for re-worming. Older dogs are usually able to throw off worms if they are in good condition when infected, but unless the puppy is given some help when he gets worms, he is likely to become seriously sick. New worm medicines containing the non-toxic but effective piperazines may be bought at your pet store or druggist's, and you can give them yourself. But remember to follow instructions carefully and do not worm the puppy unless you are sure he has worms.

If the puppy passes a long, string-like white worm in his stool or coughs one up, that is sufficient evidence, and you should proceed to worm him. Other indications are: general listlessness, a large belly, dull coat, mattery eye and coughing, but these could also be signs that your puppy is coming down with some disease. If you only *suspect* that he has worms, take him to your veterinarian for a check-up and stool examination before worming.

## THE FEMALE PUPPY

If you want to spay your female you can have it done while she is still a puppy. Her first seasonal period may occur as early as seven months, although the average Dobe female starts at about nine months. She may be spayed before or after this, or you may breed her and still spay her afterward.

The first sign of the female's being in season is a thin red discharge, which will increase for about a week, when it changes color to a thin yellowish stain, lasting about another week. Simultaneously there is a swelling of the vulva, the dog's external sexual organ. The second week is the crucial period, when she could be bred if you want her to have puppies, but it is possible for the period to be shorter or longer, so it is best not to take unnecessary risks at any time. After a third week the swelling decreases and the period is over for about six months.

The female will probably lose her puppy coat, or at least shed out part of it, about three months after she is in season, for this is the time when her puppies would be weaned if she had been mated, and females generally drop coat at that time.

If you have an absolutely climb-proof and dig-proof run within your yard, it will be safe to leave her there, but otherwise the female in season should be shut indoors. Don't leave her out alone for even a minute; she should be exercised only on leash. If you want to prevent the neighborhood dogs from hanging around your doorstep, as they inevitably will as soon as they discover that your female is in season, take her some distance away from the house before you let her relieve herself. Take her in your car to a park or field for a chance to stretch her legs. After the three weeks are up you can let her out as before, with no worry that she can have puppies until the next season. But if you want to have her spayed, consult your veterinarian about the time and age at which he prefers to do it. With a young dog the operation is simple and after a night or two at the animal hospital she can be at home, wearing only a small bandage as a souvenir.

# 4. Caring for Your Adult Doberman

## DIET

When your dog reaches his first birthday he is no longer a puppy, although he will not be fully mature and developed until he is two. For all intents and purposes, however, he may be considered full grown and adult now.

You may prefer to continue feeding your dog twice a day, although he can now eat all that he needs to be healthy at one meal a day. Usually it is best to feed that one meal, or the main meal, in the evening. Most dogs eat better this way, and digest their food better. If your dog skips an occasional meal, don't worry; after half an hour remove the food if he turns up his nose at it. Otherwise he will develop the habit of picking at his food, and food left out too long becomes stale or spoiled. If you use the dry self-feeding method, of course this does not apply.

The best indication of the correct amount to feed your dog is his state of health. A fat dog is not a healthy one; just like a fat person, he has to strain his heart—and his whole body—to carry excess weight. If you cannot give your dog more exercise, cut down on his food, and remember that those dog biscuits fed as snacks or rewards count in the calories. If your dog is thin, increase the amount and add a little more fat. You can also add flavoring he likes to pep up his appetite. The average grown dog needs 5 to 6 cups of dog meal, or a pound of canned food with an additional two cups of meal, per day. Use your own judgment for YOUR dog.

## CLEANLINESS AND GROOMING

With his short coat and clean ways, the Doberman needs little in the way of grooming. You should establish good grooming habits while your dog is a young puppy. Even though his coat is short and does not need much brushing, the puppy should learn to stand for the operation, preferably on a bench or table. When he is full grown, brushing will be easier if the dog stands quietly at a convenient height. Equipment should include a brush and hound glove.

Your pet, like all outdoor dogs, does most of his shedding in spring and

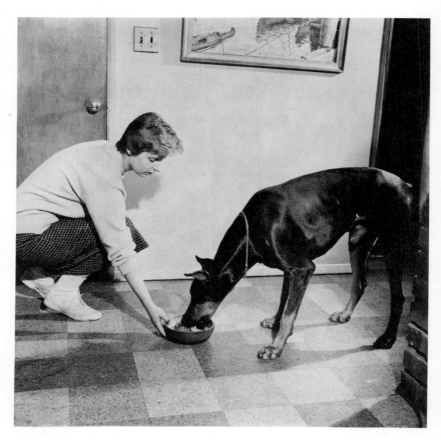

Try to feed your dog at the same time and in the same place every day. A well-balanced diet will keep him healthy and happy.

fall, although a dog that spends much of his time in the warm house will shed a little all year 'round. A vigorous brushing with a fairly stiff brush every day or two will prevent loose hair from becoming a nuisance.

Your Doberman will seldom need a bath unless he gets into something smelly or is so dirty that brushing isn't enough. When you bathe him, use one of the special dog soaps, a shampoo made for humans, or soap pieces dissolved to make a solution. Be sure to rinse all the soap out so no residue will be left to irritate the skin. Use towels to dry your Doberman afterward and, if the weather is cool, keep him in a warm place to prevent chilling. Too much bathing will dry the skin and cause shedding, so don't overdo it.

If your dog's skin is dry or if he sheds more than a few hairs in spring and fall, it may be due to lack of fat in his diet. Rub a little lanolin into his coat and add a spoonful of lard to his food. Other skin troubles, shown by scratching, redness, or a sore on the surface, should be examined by your veterinarian, who can prescribe treatment and clear up the trouble quickly. Don't delay, as once it takes hold any skin disease is hard to cure.

## NOSE, TEETH, EARS AND EYES

Normally, a dog's nose, teeth, ears and eyes need no special care. The dog's nose is cool and moist to the touch (unless he has been in a warm house); however, the "cold nose" theory is only a partial indication of health or sickness. A fever, for instance, would be shown by a hot, dry nose, but other illness might not cause this. The dog's eyes are normally bright and alert, with the eyelid down in the corner, not over the eye. If the haw is bloodshot or partially covers the eye, it may be a sign of illness or irritation. If your dog has matter in the corners of the eyes, bathe with a mild eye

If your dog's ears seem to bother him, examine them carefully and use a cotton swab to clean them.

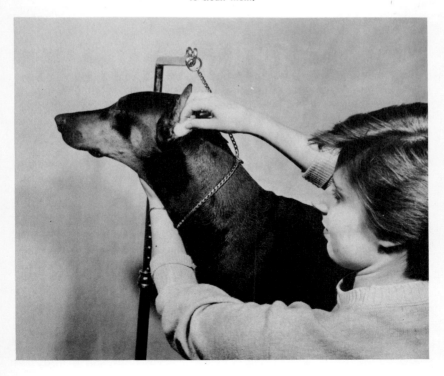

wash; obtain ointment from your veterinarian or pet shop to treat a chronic condition.

If your dog seems to have something wrong with his ears which causes him to scratch them or shake his head, cautiously probe the ear with a cotton swab. An accumulation of wax will probably work itself out. But dirt or dried blood is indicative of ear mites or infection, and should be treated immediately. Sore ears in the summer, due to fly bites, should be washed with mild soap and water, then covered with a soothing ointment, gauze-wrapped if necessary. Keep the dog protected from insects, and if necessary keep him indoors until his ears heal.

The dog's teeth will take care of themselves, although you may want your veterinarian to scrape off the unsightly tartar accumulation occasionally. A good hard bone will help to do the same thing.

## TOENAILS

Keep your dog's toenails short with a weekly clipping. Use specially designed clippers that are available at your pet shop. Never take off too much at one time, as you might cut the "quick" which is sensitive and will bleed. Cut the nails straight across, then round off the sides with a little clip or a file. Be particularly careful when you cut black nails in which the quick is not visible.

## PARASITES

If your dog picks up fleas or other skin parasites from neighbors' dogs or from the ground, weekly use of a good DDT- or Chlordane-base flea powder will get rid of them. Remember to dust his bed and change the bedding, too, as flea eggs drop off the host to hatch and wait in likely places for the dog to return. In warm weather a weekly dusting or monthly dip is good prevention.

If your grown dog is well-fed and in good health you will probably have no trouble with worms. He may pick them up from other dogs, however, so if you suspect worms, have a stool examination made and, if necessary, worm him. Fleas, too, are carriers of tapeworm, so that is one good reason to make sure the dog is free from these insects. Roundworms, the dog's most common intestinal parasite, have a life cycle which permits complete eradication by worming twice, ten days apart. The first worming will remove all adults and the second will destroy all subsequently hatched eggs before they in turn can produce more parasites.

## FIRST AID

If your dog is injured, you can give him first aid which is, in general, similar to that for a human. The same principles apply. Superficial wounds should be disinfected and healing ointment applied. If the cut is likely to

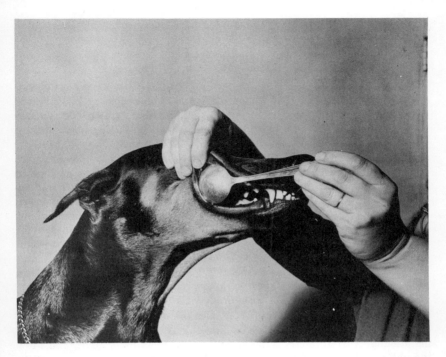

If you have to give your dog liquid medicine, hold his mouth open, pour it in, and hold his mouth closed until he swallows.

get dirty apply a bandage and restrain the dog so that he won't keep trying to remove it. A cardboard ruff will prevent him from licking his chest or body. Nails can be taped down to prevent scratching.

A board splint should be put on before moving a dog that might have a broken bone. If you are afraid that the dog will bite from pain, use a bandage muzzle made from a long strip of cloth, wrapped around the muzzle, then tied under the jaw and brought up behind the ears to hold it on. In case of severe bleeding on a limb, apply a tourniquet—a strip of cloth wrapped around a stick to tighten it will do—between the cut and the heart, but loosen it every few minutes to avoid damaging the circulation.

If you suspect that your dog has swallowed poison, try to get him to vomit by giving him salt water or mustard in water. In all these cases, rush him to your veterinarian as soon as possible, after alerting the vet by phone.

In warm weather the most important thing to remember for your dog's sake is providing fresh water. If he tends to slobber and drink too much, it may be offered at intervals of an hour or so instead of being available at all times, but it should be fresh and cool. Don't overexercise the dog or let the children play too wildly with him in the heat of the day. Don't leave him outside without shade, and never leave a dog in a car which would become overheated in the sun. It should always have some shade and ventilation through the windows.

## THE OLD DOG

With the increased knowledge and care available, there is no reason why your dog should not live to a good old age. As he grows older he may need a little additional care, however. Remember that a fat dog is not healthy, particularly as he grows older, and limit his food accordingly. The older dog needs exercise as much as ever, although his heart cannot bear the strain of sudden and violent exertion. His digestion may not be as good as it was as a puppy, so follow your veterinarian's advice about special feeding, if necessary. Failing eyesight or hearing mean lessened awareness of dangers, so you must protect him more than before. The old dog is used to his home, and to set ways, so too many strangers are bound to be a strain. For the same reason, boarding him out or a trip to the vet's are to be avoided unless absolutely necessary.

Should you decide at this time to get a puppy, to avoid being without a dog when your old retainer is no longer with you, be very careful how you introduce the puppy. He is naturally playful and will expect the older dog to respond to his advances. Sometimes the old dog will get a new lease on life from a pup. But don't make him jealous by giving to the newcomer the attention that formerly was exclusively his. Feed them apart, and show the old dog that you still love him the most; the puppy, not being used to individual attention, will not mind sharing your love.

# 5. How to Train Your Doberman Pinscher

## ANIMAL OR PET?

There is only a one-word difference between an *animal* and a *pet* and that word is TRAINING.

But training your dog depends upon many factors:

how intelligent you are;

how intelligent the dog is;

what your intentions are;

how much time you are willing to devote to the task.

First we consider the dog owner who is merely interested in training his dog to be a perfect home companion, a dog that he can be proud to own, a dog that won't embarrass him by untimely "accidents" nor kill himself by running into the street.

## THE DOG OWNER'S PART

Before you begin training your dog to be a pet, there are certain important facts to remember:

You are a human being and do not speak the same language that a dog does. So you must try to think as a pet dog thinks; your dog will try to understand you.

Training your dog is like training a child. It requires firmness tempered with kindness, strictness but gentleness, consistency, repetition and above all PATIENCE. You must have the patience to go over the training cycle time and time again until the message reaches your dog.

Did you know that a dog is the only known animal that can be bribed into learning by just a few kind words and soft pats on the back? Other animals must be bribed with food or be beaten into submission, but not your pet dog. He wants kindness and attention. Reward him with a pat on the back when he is doing well and you will soon have a dog eager to learn.

## GIVING COMMANDS

When you give commands use the shortest phrase possible and use the same word with the same meaning at all times. If you want to teach your dog to sit, then always use the word SIT. If you want your dog to lie down, then always use the word DOWN. It doesn't matter what word you use as long as your dog becomes accustomed to hearing it and acts upon it.

The trick dog that always sits on the command UP and stands at SIT was trained to obey the words that way, since words are merely sounds to him. Your dog does not understand what you say, but associates the word with his training and the tone of your voice. Unless you use commands consistently your dog will never learn to obey promptly.

## WHAT YOU WILL TEACH YOUR DOG

Your house pet should certainly learn the rudiments necessary to good behavior. Your dog should be housebroken first of all. Then he should learn how to walk properly with a collar and leash, after which he should be taught the simple commands of HEEL, SIT, COME and STAY. Only after the dog has learned these commands is it safe to train him off the leash.

Once your dog gets into the swing of his training it is wise to continue to train him in more difficult performances. After all, the hardest part of the job is establishing a communication system so that each of you learns what to expect from the other. Once your dog learns a trick or a command he will hardly ever forget it if you repeat it every so often. Begging, giving his paw, playing dead and rolling over, are entertaining tricks which you, your friends and your dog can all enjoy to mutual benefit. There are, however, more important lessons first.

## COLLAR AND LEASH

Your puppy should become used to a leash and collar at an early age. He seldom needs a license until he is six months old, and a leather collar will be outgrown several times before then. Buy one for use, not looks or permanence. A chain "choke collar" is a good substitute. Never leave a choke on a loose dog, for it could catch on something and strangle him. If you want to use one as a permanent collar, buy a clip to fasten the two ends, so that it cannot choke him.

Let the puppy wear his collar around until he is used to its feel and weight. After several short periods he will not be distracted by the strangeness and you can attach the leash. Let him pull it around and then try to lead him a bit. He will probably resist, bucking and balking, or simply sitting down and refusing to budge. Fight him for a few minutes, dragging him along if necessary, but then let him relax for the day, with plenty of affection and praise. He won't be lead-broken until he learns that he must obey the pull under any circumstance, but don't try to do it in one lesson. Ten

The "choke collar" isn't as cruel as the name implies. Because of its restraining action, it's very useful for training, but it cannot hurt your dog.

minutes a day is long enough for any training. The dog's period of concentration is short and, like a child, he will become bored if you carry it on too long.

## WHAT ABOUT LESSONS?

Try to make your training lessons interesting and appealing both to yourself and your dog. Short frequent lessons are of much more value than long lessons. It is much better for all concerned if you teach your dog for 10 minutes at a time, three times a day, than for 30 minutes once a day. The 10 minute session amuses both you and your dog and the attachment which develops between you during these lessons will be everlasting.

A good time to train your dog is for 10 minutes before you give him his breakfast; then he assumes that the meal is a reward for his being such a good dog. If you follow this schedule for all three meals your training program will be extremely successful.

## TRAINING YOUR DOG TO WALK PROPERLY

After your dog has been housebroken and has become accustomed to his collar you must teach him to walk properly on a leash. We are assuming that you will use the collar and leash when housebreaking your puppy. Once he is thoroughly familiar with the workings of these restraining objects, you must teach him to respect the master at the other end of the leash.

You should hold the leash firmly in your right hand. The dog should walk on your left side with the leash crossing the front of your body. The reason for this will be obvious once you've actually walked your dog . . . you have more control this way.

Let your dog lead you for the first few moments so that he fully understands that freedom can be his if he goes about it properly. He know already that when he wants to go outdoors the leash and collar are necessary, so he has respect for the leash. Now, if while walking he starts to pull in one direction, all you do is *stop walking*. He will walk a few steps and then find that he can't walk any further. He will then turn and look into your face. *This is the crucial point.* Just stand there for a moment and stare right back at him . . . Now walk another 10 feet and stop again. Again your dog will probably walk out the leash, find he can't go any further, and turn around and look again. If he starts to pull and jerk then just stand there. After he quiets down, just bend down and comfort him as he may be frightened. Keep up this training until he learns not to outwalk you.

You must understand that most dogs like to stop and sniff around a bit until they find THE place to do their duty. Be kind enough to stop and wait. This is the whole story . . . it's as easy as that. A smart dog can learn to walk properly in a few days, provided you have taught him correctly from the beginning. A dog that is incorrectly trained initially may take a month to retrain, but in any event, every dog can earn to walk properly on a leash!

## TRAINING YOUR DOG TO COME TO YOU

Your dog has been named and he knows his name. After hearing his name called over and over again in your home, he finds that it pays to come when called. Why? Because you only call him when his food is ready or when you wish to play with him and pet him. Outside the house it is a different story. He would rather play by himself or with other dogs or chase a cat than play with you. So, he must be trained to come to you when he is called. Here's how to do it:

After you have trained your pet to walk properly on a leash let him walk out the entire length of the leash. Then stop and call him to you. If he just

With good training, your Doberman will stand alertly, waiting for your next command.

stands there looking up with those soulful eyes that made you buy him in the first place, then gently pull on the leash until he comes to your feet, even if you have to drag him over. By no means should you walk to him! Pat his head, making a big fuss over him as though you haven't seen him for weeks!

Then walk along and try it all over again. Repeat the process until he finally gets the idea. It shouldn't take long if you are consistent about it every time you take him out for his walk.

## TRAINING YOUR DOG TO STAY AT YOUR SIDE

From here on, the training gets a bit more difficult. So far the housebreaking, walking and coming when called has constituted the basic training EVERY dog must know. What follows is more difficult to teach and is harder for the dog to learn because it means he has to give up some of his freedom and playfulness.

To train your dog to stay by your side is a little harder than to train him not to pull on the leash. For the "heel" training, the choke chain collar, designed to tighten about your dog's neck if he pulls too hard, is a necessity. The collar is definitely not a cruel instrument (as the name might imply). Here's what you do:

Put the choke chain collar on your dog the next time you take him out. If he pulls too hard, this type collar will definitely break that habit one, two, three! Once you've gotten him accustomed to the action of the choke chain collar stop the walk and start out again with the dog's nose even with your left knee. Walk quickly, repeating as you go the word HEEL over and over again. If your dog walks out past your knee, jerk him back firmly, but not *cruelly*, raising your voice HEEL at the same time. If he persists in going out in front of you all the time, stop and start all over again. Repeat this process until he learns it. Have patience, for once he learns to walk by your side you will have a well-mannered dog all his life.

Some dogs are a bit lazy and will walk behind you instead of in front of you. If your dog does this, stop and call him to you and keep calling him with the word HEEL until he finally gets the idea. Keep your dog informed that the word HEEL means he is to walk close to your left heel.

After your dog has learned to HEEL on a tight lead, you can use a slack leash and let him wear a leather collar if you prefer. If he forgets himself, put the choke chain collar on again right away. Don't give him a chance to forget his lessons . . . and don't forget to use the same word HEEL at all times.

## TRAINING YOUR DOG TO STOP WITHOUT COMMAND

When your dog has been trained to HEEL on a loose leash, the next step in his training is to STOP without command so that if you stop at a street corner or to talk to someone along the way, your dog doesn't pull you

You can be very proud of your dog (and yourself) when he learns to sit in heel position.

to get going. Training to stop without command requires use of the choke chain collar for the first lessons.

Take your dog out for his usual walk, keeping him at HEEL all the time. Then stop dead in your tracks keeping the leash tight in your hands without a bit of slack. DO NOT LET HIM SIT DOWN! No command is necessary. As soon as he stops, pat him on the back and give him some dog candy. Then walk on again briskly and stop short. Keep your dog on the tight leash at all times and repeat this until he learns that he must stop dead in his tracks just as you do. When you stop, stop *deliberately* so that he can actually anticipate your stopping and be with you at all times. You can tell when he is being attentive for he will walk a few steps and then turn his head so that he can keep an eye on your face. He will actually crave to satisfy you once he has

To teach your Doberman to sit and stay, use both voice and hand signals.

been properly taught, and he will only take a few steps before he swings his head to look at you. Next time you see a well-trained dog walking along the street, notice how much time he spends looking at his master instead of at other things.

Once your dog has learned to stop without command and you want to walk again, you can signal him by many means. One way is to slacken your leash and then start walking so that he will learn that a slackened leash means you intend to walk again. Another way is to signal him verbally with the word "Go" or "Come on Pal" or something similar to that. It doesn't matter what word you use as long as you use the same word all the time.

## OFF-THE-LEASH TRAINING

After your dog has accomplished these lessons it is time to begin his training without a leash. Try to find a large open area which is fenced in. If no such area is available, find as quiet a street as you can (even late at night so that few automobiles are around) and begin your training there.

Let's assume that your dog heels and stops without command. After you've walked him a few feet and tested him on stopping without command, bend down and remove the leash. Start walking briskly as you did when training him to heel. Stop suddenly without command and see if he does the same. If he doesn't, then immediately snap on the leash with the choke collar and go through the training again. Walk once with the leash on and once with the leash off, until finally your dog gets the idea that he can have more freedom by behaving himself.

## TRAINING YOUR DOG TO SIT

After a brisk walk go through the previous lessons as far as the short stop. Your dog will be standing watching you and waiting for the loose leash to walk on further. When you reach this point, gently push his hindquarters down with your left hand as you hold the leash tightly raised in your right hand. This will keep his head up and his butt down. Don't let him lie all the way down or cower. Use just enough pressure so he knows that he's to sit. Once he's in the sitting position give him a few pats on the head and start walking again.

Do this several times. He should go into the sitting position every time you want him to.

Remember that when you stopped your dog was standing at your side ready to go off again whenever you were ready. Now use the word SIT very often so he can accustom his ears to *that* sound. Every time you push his hindquarters down, say SIT. Keep repeating this word over and over again as you push him down. Soon he will learn when he should sit and when he should stay close to your side when you stop for a short time.

After thoroughly training your dog in sitting with a leash, go through the same method of training without a leash. A simple method is to walk along briskly, stop and tell him to SIT. As soon as he sits take the leash off and walk again. Then stop and tell him to SIT again.

If he doesn't sit upon command, hold his choke chain in your hand and force his hindquarters down into the sitting position. Do this again and again until he learns. It is always important to keep in mind that you must never start a new lesson until the old one is mastered. Inconsistency on your part is considered a weakness by your dog.

## TRAINING YOUR DOG TO LIE DOWN

Now that your dog can sit with a leash or without a leash and is thoroughly familiar with your training routine, perhaps you want to train him to lie down. Many people feel that there is no reason for teaching him to lie down and they don't bother, but if you want him to ride safely in an automobile, training in lying down is important.

Usually DOWN is the command word for lying down although any word you use will be acceptable, provided you use the same word every time.

Take your dog out and go through the training sequence until you have him in a sitting position. Then walk in front of him and gently pull his two front paws forward so that he automatically falls into the lying down position. As you do this say DOWN. If he raises his hindquarters then use the command SIT and his hindquarters should drop immediately. Only constant repetition of this exercise will finally get him to lie down immediately upon command.

It is very helpful to use a hand signal along with the verbal command DOWN. The usual hand signal is to extend your left hand, with your palm down, as a sign to lie down. A very successful variation is merely to point down as you give the order. Any signal is satisfactory as long as you are consistent.

When giving the hand signal be careful that your dog doesn't think you are threatening him.

## TRAINING YOUR DOG TO STAY

The main objective in teaching your dog to sit and lie down is to get him to stay where you want him. Many times you will restrict him to a certain room, possibly the kitchen. When the front door rings, you don't want him tracking through the house. Will you have to lock him in the kitchen before you open the front door? Do you want him to follow you all over the house whenever you move from room to room? If the answer to these questions is to be "No!" then he must be trained to stay.

Then again, what more beautiful sight is there than to see a dog "parked" outside a supermarket waiting in a sitting or lying down position. Nothing but his master's command can budge him. Though strangers may pat him and entice him, nothing can make him move from the position he is in. These are some of the rewards you receive from training.

To train your dog to stay is not a difficult feat at all. Once he sits or lies upon command, proceed with the STAY command. Immediately after he is seated (or lying down) drop the leash and walk away three or four steps. Keep facing him while you are doing this, and, if he starts to rise to follow you, raise your voice and give the hand signal DOWN! If he doesn't get down immediately, walk back to him very briskly and force him down in no uncertain manner. Then try again to walk a few feet from him. Repeat this sequence until he finally stays at the command. The following day walk a

Extend your left hand, palm down, as you tell your Doberman to lie down.

little bit further; keep up this training until finally you can walk away, out of sight, and he will stay where he is, waiting for you.

When you want your dog to rise out of the position he is in, command COME (or call his name, whichever way you have decided earlier in his training). Do not allow him to run to you from the STAY position because you return to his line of vision. He must await your permission to come to you. This part of the training either makes or breaks a dog. The test is simple for an obedient, well disciplined dog. If you are lax and inconsistent in the initial stages, then it will be impossible to train him to stay.

Time out for relaxation! Even though your dog will enjoy his training, he'll welcome some time just devoted to play.

## DISCIPLINE TRAINING FOR YOUR DOG

Up to this point you have been training your dog to act upon command. Now you will attempt to train his intelligence. This is another important part of the training problem and it is the part that separates a "smart" dog from one that doesn't "use his head."

All dogs, regardless of their training, will get the urge to run after another dog, to chase a cat, to fetch, or just to run for the sheer love of running. In the open field or park this is perfectly all right, but in the city it can be catastrophic! Let's assume that your dog has a bad habit of slipping off his collar and making a mad dash away from you. You may find this out some fine, bright morning when both of you are in fine spirits: He will spot a cat, and without warning will dash off, either pulling the leash right out of your unwary hands or slipping his head out of the collar. A moment of panic will hit you both. But, once the initial impact of the moment is over, he will come scampering back at the command COME.

*At this point do not beat your dog.* He knows he has done something wrong and he is a bit confused himself. Just pat him on the head and ignore it . . . *this time.* Then walk back to the house and get a long rope, 25 to 30 feet long. Tie this rope to his regular collar (do not use a choke chain) and also use the regular leash. Try to get your dog into the same situation as the one he bolted from. When he runs away from you again (if he does), drop the leash but hold onto the rope. When he gets far enough away give a loud holler STOP and jerk the rope at the same time. He will spin in his tracks and lay where he is, thoroughly confused and a bit scared.

Go over to him and make a big fuss over him as though you can't imagine what happened. Tell him he should never have left your side. Repeat this training four or five times and he will never bolt from you again.

You can practice the command STOP by running a few steps with him and then shouting the command STOP as you suddenly stop short. By repeating the command STOP in every such situation it won't be too long before you can make your dog STOP on a dime!

**Even though children and dogs make a pretty picture, you should not let your dog get into the sitting-on-furniture habit.**

Teach your dog not to jump on you or anyone else. Even your dog-loving friends will not enjoy such friendliness in a dog the size of your Doberman.

## KEEPING YOUR DOG OFF THE FURNITURE

Your favorite sofa or chair will also be your dog's favorite seat. It is naturally used the most and so will have the odors (which only your dog can smell) of the beloved master. There are two ways of training your dog out of the habit of sitting in your chair.

The simplest way of breaking the habit is to soak a small rag with a special dog scent which is repulsive to dogs. Put the rag on the chair which your dog favors. He will jump on the chair, get a whiff of the scent and make a detour of the chair forever more!

Another way to train is to pull him off the chair every time you catch him there and immediately command him to lie DOWN at your feet. Then give him a severe tongue lashing. After a few times he will never go to the chair again WHILE YOU ARE AROUND! The greater problem is to teach him to stay away all the time. The usual plan is to get a few inexpensive mouse traps and set them (without bait of course) with a few sheets of newspaper over them. As soon as your dog jumps onto the chair the mousetrap goes SNAP and off the chair goes the dog. He may try it again, but then the second trap will go off, and he will have learned his lesson.

Since your dog has his own bed, train him to stay in it when you don't want him to be any place else. This can be done by saying the word BED in a loud voice and dragging him over and placing him in it. Do this a few times and he will learn where to go when you want him in bed!

## TRAINING YOUR DOG NOT TO BARK

For people who live close to another family, a barking dog is a nuisance and your dog must be trained not to bark unless he hears a very strange sound or sees a stranger on your premises. Do not forget that barking is to a dog what a voice is to a human and he expresses happiness, alarm, pain and warning in his bark. It would be impossible to write down all the different sounds that a dog can make, but you will recognize the difference between a whimper, a growl, a howl and a bark. A whimper denotes pain or discomfort. A growl denotes danger and is a warning. A howl denotes loneliness and a bark denotes strange sounds.

To break your dog of excess barking merely requires the use of a rolled newspaper. Every time he barks for some unknown reason, or barks excessively when strangers approach, swat your own hand smartly with the rolled paper, making as loud a smack as possible and at the same time command QUIET. This has never failed to stop a dog. You must repeat this every time he barks.

## TRAINING YOUR DOG NOT TO JUMP ON PEOPLE

Some dogs are so affectionate that they will jump on everybody who comes into sight in order to get their attention and affection. Only you can train your dog not to jump. As he jumps up to greet *you*, merely bend your knee so he hits it with his chest and falls over. He cannot see your knee coming up as his head will be above your knee. After a few falls he will get the idea that it isn't practical to jump up to greet you or anyone.

Of course if he has learned the meaning of the command DOWN, then use that command when he jumps up.

## TRAINING YOUR DOG TO DO TRICKS

Nearly every housedog learns a few tricks without training during the course of his puppyhood. These are usually accidentally learned, but the master observes the dog doing them and then prompts him to repeat the same thing over and over again.

You will deliberately want to train your dog to shake hands. First get him into the sitting position. Then upon the command PAW, lift his paw in your hand and shake it vigorously without knocking him off balance. Then praise him. Repeat this several times a day and in a week he will all but hold out his paw when you walk in the door!

**It's hard to chase the puppy off the chair when he looks so comfortable, but this is a time when firmness is necessary.**

Ch. Steb's Top Skipper, a Westminster and Working Group Winner, poses proudly in front of his well-deserved trophies.

Teaching your dog to beg is done in the same manner. Place him in the sitting position with the proper command. Then lift his front paws up until he is in a begging position. Hold him that way until he finds a comfortable balance and then let him balance himself. As he gets his balance, hold a piece of dog candy right over his nose. As soon as you let go of his front paws, lower the dog candy to his mouth and let him take it from your hands. Hold the dog candy firmly so it takes a few seconds for him to pry it loose. During this time you are saying BEG, over and over. From then on, you must bribe him with dog candy until he assumes the begging position upon the command BEG. Reward him whenever he obeys.

Your dog can learn to beg, too. First hold him in position, then let go when he has
balanced himself. Soon he will beg on command.

Training a dog is easy enough for a child to do. All it takes is patience, consistency and firmness.

# 6. Caring for the Female and Raising Puppies

Whether or not you bought your female dog intending to breed her, some preparation is necessary when and if you decide to take this step.

## WHEN TO BREED

It is usually best to breed on the second or third season. Plan in advance the time of year which is best for you, taking into account where the puppies will be born and raised. You will keep them until they are at least six weeks old, and a litter of husky pups takes up considerable space by then. Other considerations are selling the puppies (Christmas vs. springtime sales), your own vacation, and time available to care for them. You'll need at least an hour a day to feed and clean up after the mother and puppies but probably it will take you much longer — with time out to admire and play with them!

## CHOOSING THE STUD

You can plan to breed your female about 6½ months after the start of her last season, although a variation of a month or two either way is not unusual. Choose the stud dog and make arrangements well in advance. If you are breeding for show stock, which may command better prices, a mate should be chosen with an eye to complementing the deficiencies of your female. If possible, the dogs should have several ancestors in common within the last two or three generations, as such combinations generally "click" best. The male should have a good show record or be the sire of show winners if old enough to be proven.

The owner of such a male usually charges a fee for the use of the dog. This does not guarantee a litter, but you generally have the right to breed your female again if she does not have puppies. In some cases the owner of the stud will agree to take a choice puppy in place of a stud fee. You should settle all details beforehand, including the possibility of a single surviving puppy, deciding the age at which he is to make his choice and take the pup, and so on.

If you want to raise a litter "just for the fun of it" and plan merely to

When you bathe your Doberman, be sure to rinse all the soap out and dry him thoroughly.

make use of an available male, the most important selection point is temperament. Make sure the dog is friendly as well as healthy, because a bad disposition could appear in his puppies, and this is the worst of all traits in a dog destined to be a pet. In such cases a "stud fee puppy," not necessarily the choice of the litter, is the usual payment.

## PREPARATION FOR BREEDING

Before you breed your female, make sure she is in good health. She should be neither too thin nor too fat. Any skin disease *must* be cured before it can be passed on to the puppies. If she has worms she should be wormed before being bred or within three weeks afterward. It is generally considered a good idea to revaccinate her against distemper and hepatitis before the puppies are born. This will increase the immunity the puppies receive during their early, most vulnerable period.

The female will probably be ready to breed 12 days after the first colored discharge. You can usually make arrangements to board her with the owner of the male for a few days, to insure her being there at the proper time, or you can take her to be mated and bring her home the same day. If she still appears receptive she may be bred again two days later. However, some females never show signs of willingness, so it helps to have the experience of a breeder. Usually the second day after the discharge changes color is the proper time, and she may be bred for about three days following. For an additional week or so she may have some discharge and attract other dogs by her odor, but can seldom be bred.

## THE FEMALE IN WHELP

You can expect the puppies nine weeks from the day of breeding, although 61 days is as common as 63. During this time the female should receive normal care and exercise. If she was overweight, don't increase her food at first; excess weight at whelping time is bad. If she is on the thin side build her up, giving some milk and biscuit at noon if she likes it. You may add one of the mineral and vitamin supplements to her food to make sure that the puppies will be healthy. As her appetite increases, feed her more. During the last two weeks the puppies grow enormously and she will probably have little room for food and less appetite. She should be tempted with meat, liver and milk, however.

As the female in whelp grows heavier, cut out violent exercise and jumping. Although a dog used to such activities will often play with the children or run around voluntarily, restrain her for her own sake.

## PREPARING FOR THE PUPPIES

Prepare a whelping box a few days before the puppies are due, and allow the mother to sleep there overnight or to spend some time in it during the day to become accustomed to it. Then she is less likely to try to have her pups under the front porch or in the middle of your bed. A variety of places will serve, such as a corner of your cellar, garage, or an unused room. If the weather is warm, a large outdoor doghouse will do, well protected from rain or draft. A whelping box serves to separate mother and puppies from visitors and other distractions. The walls should be high enough to restrain the puppies, yet allow the mother to get away from the puppies after she has fed them. Four feet square is minimum size, and one-foot walls will keep the pups in until they begin to climb, when the walls should be built up. Then the puppies really need more room anyway, so double the space with a very low partition down the middle and you will find them naturally housebreaking themselves.

As the female in whelp grows heavier, don't let her indulge in too much excited play.

Layers of newspaper spread over the whole area will make excellent bedding and be absorbent enough to keep the surface warm and dry. They should be removed daily and replaced with another thick layer. An old quilt or washable blanket makes better footing for the nursing puppies than slippery newspaper during the first week, and is softer for the mother.

Be prepared for the actual whelping several days in advance. Usually the female will tear up papers, refuse food and generally act restless. These may be false alarms; the real test is her temperature, which will drop to below 100° about 12 hours before whelping. Take it with a rectal thermometer morning and evening, and when the temperature goes down put her in the pen, looking in on her frequently.

Their taped ears don't prevent the puppies from looking for someone to play with.

## WHELPING

Usually little help is needed but it is wise to stay close to make sure that the mother's lack of experience does not cause an unnecessary accident. Be ready to help when the first puppy arrives, for it could smother if the mother does not break the membrane enclosing it. She should start right away to lick the puppy, drying and stimulating it, but you can do it with a soft rough towel instead. The afterbirth should follow the birth of each puppy, attached to the puppy by the long umbilical cord. Watch to make sure that each is expelled, for retaining this material can cause infection. In her instinct for cleanliness the mother will probably eat the afterbirth after biting the cord. One or two will not hurt her; they stimulate milk supply as well as labor for remaining pups. But too many can make her lose appetite for the food she needs to feed her pups and regain her strength. So remove the rest of them along with the wet newspapers and keep the pen dry and clean to relieve her anxiety.

If the mother does not bite the cord, or does it too close to the body, take over the job, to prevent an umbilical hernia. Tearing is recommended, but you can cut it, about two inches from the body, with a sawing motion of scissors that have been sterilized in alcohol. Then dip the end of the cord in a shallow dish of iodine; the cord will dry up and fall off in a few days.

The puppies should follow each other at intervals of not more than one hour. If more time goes past and you are sure there are still pups to come, a brisk walk outside may start labor again. If your dog is actively straining without producing a puppy it may be presented backward, a so-called "breech" or upside-down birth. Careful assistance with a well-soaped finger to feel for the puppy or ease it back may help, but never attempt to pull it by force against the mother. This could cause serious damage, so let an expert handle it.

If anything seems wrong, waste no time in calling your veterinarian who can examine her and if necessary give hormones which will bring the remaining puppies. You may want his experience in whelping the litter even if all goes well. He will probably prefer to have the puppies born at his hospital rather than to get up in the middle of the night to come to your home. The mother would, no doubt, prefer to stay at home, but you can be sure she will get the best of care in his hospital. If the puppies are born at home and all goes as it should, watch the mother carefully afterward. It is wise to have the veterinarian check her and the pups, anyway, and remove the puppies' dewclaws and dock their tails when they are two to four days old.

## RAISING THE PUPPIES

Hold each puppy to a breast as soon as he is dry, for a good meal without competition. Then he may join his littermates in a basket out of his mother's way while she is whelping. Keep a supply of evaporated milk on hand for emergencies, or later weaning. A formula of evaporated milk, corn syrup and a little water with egg yolk should be warmed and fed in a doll or baby bottle if necessary. A supplementary feeding often helps weak pups over the hump. Keep track of birth weights, and take weekly readings thereafter for an accurate record of the pups' growth and health.

After the puppies have arrived, take the mother outside for a walk and drink, and then leave her to take care of them. She will probably not want to stay away more than a minute or two for the first few weeks. Be sure to keep water available at all times, and feed her milk or broth frequently, as she needs liquids to produce milk. Encourage her to eat by giving her her favorite foods, until she asks for food of her own accord. She will soon develop a ravenous appetite and should have at least two large meals a day, with dry food available in addition.

Prepare a warm place to put the puppies to keep them dry and help them to a good start in life. You can use a cardboard box in which you put an electric heating pad or hot water bottle covered with flannel. Set the box near the mother so that she can see her puppies. She will usually allow you to help, but don't take the puppies out of sight. Let her handle things if your interference seems to make her nervous.

Be sure that all the puppies are getting enough to eat. If the mother sits or stands instead of lying still to nurse, the probable cause is scratching from the puppies' nails. You can remedy this by clipping them, as you do hers. Manicure scissors will do for these tiny claws.

Some breeders advise disposing of the smaller or weaker pups in a large litter, since the mother has trouble in handling more than six or seven. But you can help her out by preparing an extra puppy box or basket. Leave half the litter with the mother and the other half in a warm place, changing off at two-hour intervals at first. Later you may change the pups less frequently, leaving them all together except during the day. Try supplementary feeding, too; as soon as their eyes open, at about two weeks, they will lap from a dish, anyway.

## WEANING THE PUPPIES

The puppies should normally be completely weaned at five weeks, although you start to feed them at three weeks. They will find it easier to lap semi-solid food than to drink milk at first, so mix baby cereal with whole or evaporated milk, warmed to body temperature, and offer it to the puppies in a saucer. Until they learn to lap, it is best to feed one or two at a time, because they are more likely to walk into it than to eat. Hold the saucer at chin level, and let them gather around, keeping paws out of the dish. A damp sponge afterward prevents most of the cereal from sticking to their skin if the mother doesn't clean them up. Once they have gotten the idea, broth or babies' meat soup may be alternated with milk, and you can start them on finely chopped meat. At four weeks they will eat four meals a day, and soon do without their mother entirely. Start them on mixed dog food, or leave it with them in a dish for self-feeding. Don't leave water with them all the time; at this age everything is to play with and they will use it as a wading pool. They can drink all they need if it is offered several times a day, after meals.

As the puppies grow up the mother will go into the pen only to nurse them, first sitting up and then standing. To dry her up completely, keep her away from the puppies for longer periods; after a few days of part-time nursing she can stay away for still longer periods, and then completely. The little milk left will be resorbed.

The puppies may be put outside, unless it is too cold, as soon as their eyes are open, and will benefit from the sunlight and vitamins. Provide a box with a rubber mat or newspapers on the bottom to protect them from cold or damp. At six weeks they can go outside permanently unless it is very cold, but make sure that they go into their shelter at night or in bad weather. By

Your dog may try to convince you that he's starving, but you know better. A firm "no" will keep him from being a nuisance at the table.

now cleaning up is a man-sized job, so put them out at least during the day and make your task easier. Be sure to clean their run daily, as worms and other infections are lurking. You can expect the pups to need at least one worming before they are ready to go to new homes, so take a stool sample to your veterinarian before they are three weeks old. If one puppy has worms all should be wormed. Follow the veterinarian's advice, and this applies also to vaccination. If you plan to keep a pup you will want to vaccinate him at the earliest age, so his littermates should be done at the same time.

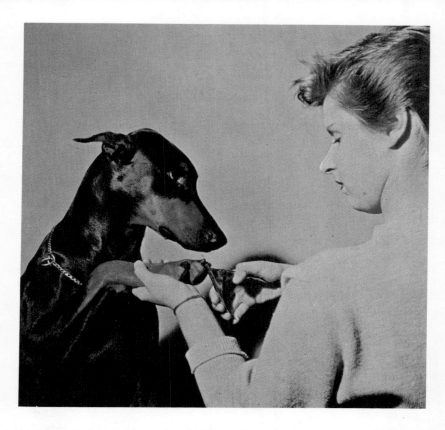

Your Doberman's toenails need a weekly clipping, with specially designed clippers. Cut the nails straight across, being careful not to cut the quick.

## CROPPING THE PUPPIES' EARS

Most veterinarians prefer to crop ears at about eight weeks, with three months the outside age limit. This is really a job for the expert, since a dog's appearance is greatly affected by his ears. After-care is very important, so follow the vet's instructions. Of course cropping is not required, even for the show ring, and is not allowed in some states, but an uncropped Doberman is rarely seen in this country — it is merely a matter of fashion.

If your dog's ears are cropped by an expert, they will stand erect and improve his appearance.

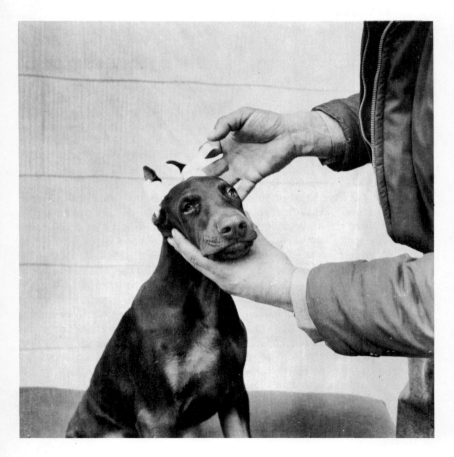

# 7. Showing Your Doberman Pinscher

As your puppy grows he will doubtless have many admirers among your friends, some of whom are bound to say, "Oh, what a handsome dog —you should certainly show him!" Perhaps even a breeder or judge will say he has show possibilities, and although you didn't buy him with that thought in mind, "Cinderella" champions do come along now and then— often enough to keep dog breeders perennially optimistic.

If you do have ideas of showing your dog, get the opinion of someone with experience first. With favorable criticism, go ahead with your plans to show him. For the novice dog and handler, sanction shows are a good way to gain ring poise and experience. These are small shows often held by the local kennel club or breed specialty club. Entry fees are low and paid at the door, breeds and sexes are usually judged together, and the prizes and ribbons are not important. They provide a good opportunity to learn what goes on at a show, and to conquer ring nervousness. Matches are usually held during the evening or on a weekend afternoon, and you need stay only to be judged.

Before you go to a show your dog should be trained to gait at a trot beside you, with head up and in a straight line. In the ring you will have to gait around the edge with other dogs and then individually up and down the center runner. In addition the dog must stand for examination by the judge, who will look at him closely and feel his head and body structure. He should be taught to stand squarely, hind feet slightly back, head and tail up on the alert. He must hold the pose when you place his feet and show animation for a piece of boiled liver in your hand or a toy mouse thrown in front of you.

If you plan to show your Doberman, train him to stand still, with his legs placed squarely, hind feet slightly back.

## ADVANCE PREPARATION

Entries close about two weeks in advance for the larger or "point" shows. You can obtain the dates of coming shows in your vicinity by writing to the Gaines Dog Research Center, 250 Park Ave., New York 17, N. Y. You will probably want to enter your dog in novice class, or in puppy class if he is between six and twelve months.

The day before the benched point show, pack your kit. You will want to take a water dish and bottle of water for your dog (so that he won't be affected by a change in drinking water, and you won't have to go look for it). Also take a chain or leash to fasten him to the bench or stall where he must remain during the show, and a show lead, as well as grooming tools. The show lead is a thin nylon or cord collar and leash combined, which does not detract from the dog's appearance as much as a clumsier chain and lead. Also put in the identification ticket sent by the show superintendent, noting the time you must be there and place where the show will be held, as well as time of judging.

If you have kept your dog's coat in good condition, there is little to do the day before the show. Groom him thoroughly to remove dust and loose hairs and to make his coat gleam. Cut or file his toenails short and trim his whiskers and eyebrows close so his face appears smooth.

Don't feed your dog the morning of the show, or give him at most a light meal. He will be more comfortable in the car on the way, and will show more enthusiastically. When you arrive at the show grounds an official veterinarian will check your dog for health, and then you should find his bench and settle him there.

## THE SHOW

Take your dog to the exercise ring to relieve himself, and give him a final grooming, then wait at the ring for your class to be called. All male classes are first, in this order: puppy, novice, bred by exhibitor. American-bred, open.

The winners compete for Winners Dog, who is awarded points toward his championship according to the number present. The winner competes against the best female, then against champions entered in "specials only" for best of breed. The next step is the Working group, where the best Doberman will compete against other breeds including Boxers, Collies and German Shepherds, and the winner there goes on to compete for Best in Show against the Sporting, Hound, Terrier, Toy and Non-Sporting winners.

Another aspect of dog shows is the obedience trial. Any purebred dog may compete, to be judged on performance instead of conformation. There are three classes of increasing difficulty: novice, open and utility, leading to the degrees of C.D., C.D.X. and U.D.—companion dog (excellent) and utility dog. Tracking, or trailing, tests are also held.

If your dog has received the training we have described previously, he is well on the way to the necessary requirements for the novice class, and you may wish to continue. There are many obedience classes where an experienced trainer can help you with your dog; classes are held weekly at a nominal fee. It helps to accustom the dog to behaving in the company of others, but a daily training period at home is also necessary. For the novice class your dog must heel on and off leash, stand for examination, come when

This alert Doberman is confident he'll win a prize — and he's right.

called, sit with you at the end of the ring for one minute, and lie down for three minutes. In advanced trials, retrieving, jumps, longer stays, and more difficult tasks are added. Attending an obedience class is excellent training for the show ring, or for a well-behaved dog you will be proud to own.

If you have kept your dog's coat in good condition, all you have to do is brush him before the show.

Heeling, both on and off leash, is required of novice dogs in obedience trials.

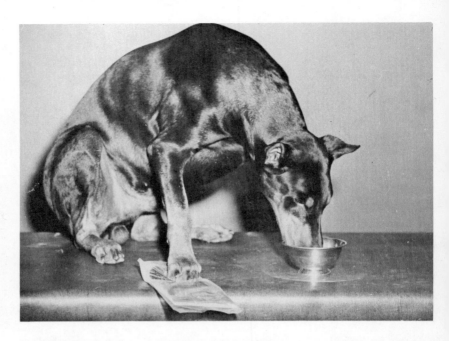

Ch. Steb's Top Skipper keeps a firm paw on the Westminster rosette he won, as he eats from his silver bowl, another prize.